CW00917367

Simon Gray

Simon Gray was born in 1936 in Hayling Island.
He lives in London with his wife, Victoria, two cats
and two dogs.

SIMON GRAY

Little Nell

inspired by Claire Tomalin's book
The Invisible Woman
The Story of Nelly Ternan and Charles Dickens

faber and faber

First published in 2006
by Faber and Faber Limited
3 Queen Square, London WC1N 3AU

Typeset by Country Setting, Kingsdown, Kent CT14 8ES
Printed in England by Bookmarque, Croydon, Surrey

A CIP record for this book
is available from the British Library

ISBN 978-0-571-23424-0
0-571-23424-0

2 4 6 8 10 9 7 5 3 1

For Simon Callow

Introduction

Decades ago, when Peter Hall was running the National Theatre, he said he'd like to commission a play from me; had I anything in mind? I said yes, I'd longed for years to write a sort of psychological and theatrical epic about Dickens, but had kept postponing it because even if I managed to write it I couldn't conceive of its ever being produced: it would require an enormous cast and complicated sets, and would be very expensive. He said that the National would be able to provide the cast and sets, and encouraged me to take a crack at it, adding that he might direct it himself.

A few days after this conversation, when I had a long gap between seminars – in those days I was a lecturer in English Literature at Queen Mary College – I sat down at my desk, opened a pad and began to write. That night, at home, I typed up what I'd written, and then went on from there, and on, late into the night. Over the next few weeks, writing in pencil during the day and typing in the evenings, I went hard at it, and made great progress, it seemed to me, almost as if the story had been waiting for me, fully formed – all I had to do was to keep doing what I was doing and I would be there in no time, or at least have a first draft from which I could then proceed at leisure.

I'd got to just before the end of the first act when a cheque arrived from my agent for what was then quite a substantial sum of money. It was the advance from the National Theatre for a play on the life of Charles Dickens, to be delivered in a year's time – the precise date was specified – for production on the Olivier stage. I had never before in my writing life accepted money for work not yet done – all my stage plays had been uncommissioned, and when offered a commission for a television play I always asked for a couple of weeks 'to think about it', then immediately set about writing it, and only after I'd finished it would I accept the commission to begin it. I'd like to think that this behaviour was from principle, a high-minded belief that inspiration would be poisoned by commerce, but really it was from a fear that I couldn't really cut it in a world of advances and deadlines, as real playwrights do.

The fact is that I have always had difficulty in thinking of myself as a playwright. In the space on official forms where you have to put down your occupation I kept on putting down 'Lecturer' long after I'd given up lecturing, and now that that's visibly implausible and I'm afraid that I'd be asked where, and to whom, I put 'Writer' in a loose sort of way, with a little gap between the 'i' and the 't' and a sort of squiggle in it. Wri~ter.

I can't write when I'm afraid to write. If I force myself I become self-conscious, and then I feel bogus, and then I feel ashamed. Not writing, on the other hand, makes me feel that I'm being stolen from, although I don't know by whom, unless it's by time, of course. Or TIME . . .

I decided to give up on the play for a while, get stuck into something else.

Stuck into what? My sense of failure with Dickens lapped into whatever I was writing, as if I were doomed to keep on repeating the experience, though in increasingly minor keys – failed attempts to convert my old stage plays into television films, for instance, or to convert my old television films into stage plays. Furthermore, I blamed Dickens for my inability to write a play about him, coming close to hating him, especially when he was the subject of a seminar. When I read out paragraphs from his novels to illustrate his vitality, his range of tone, his gymnastic jumps from melodrama to tomfoolery and back again, the sheer inimitability of the Inimitable, so forth, so forth, my voice would become feeble and whiny, running against the great-hearted spirit of his prose in spiteful counterpoint – I would have either to falter away into humdrum commentary, deploying the routine Cambridge–Leavis terminology – 'great creative genius' , 'completely and fully and richly on the side of life', etc. – or would close the book with theatrical abruptness, and go into reverential dumb-show, raising my hands to the surrender position, working my rather bushy eyebrows, pursing and unpursing my lips like a blowfish. I wonder what effect these displays had on my students all those years ago. Did I succeed in putting them off Dickens for life, as was possibly my unconscious aim?

Realising that both my careers were in rapid decline, I did the only thing I could think to do, which was to return the advance. It was a very significant moment in my life, although I'm sure it was a completely insignificant one in the life of the National Theatre – in fact I doubt if anyone except the accountants noticed, though I remember Peter Hall asking me a month or so later, when I bumped into him at something or other, how the Dickens play was coming on, and having the politeness to appear disappointed when I explained that what with my teaching commitments, plus all the College administration, on top of which my young children, etc., I'd been compelled to give it up for a while.

Now and then, when I thought it wasn't looking, I had a few stabs at tackling it – oddly aggressive imagery now I look at the words, 'stabbing' and 'tackling' to describe an attempt to write a play, but possibly accurate in that I felt sure that I would only manage it by violence and deceit, pretending, when I sat down to the typewriter, that I had hundreds of alternative projects, then suddenly let fly, batter, batter, batter at the typewriter: 'Come out, you bastard! Come out and fight!' sort of stuff.

About thirty-five years later, or about five years ago, to look at it from the other way around, Simon Callow asked me over one of our regular dinners whether I knew *The Invisible Woman*, Claire Tomalin's book about Dickens's long affair with the actress Ellen Ternan, I said yes, I'd read it and admired it when it first came out: it was such an elegant and eloquent account of the sapping logistics of adultery that it had made me realise how deeply he must have cared for her. It had been far more than an affair, it had been a marriage, really, a secret marriage. Yes, Simon said, and potentially very dramatic; he'd been trying to set up a television film based on it but with no luck so far. Would I be interested in doing a script?

I now loved Dickens once more, but the thought of tangling with him as a writer rather than just as a reader made me nervous – I feared that I might turn an old scar into a fresh wound. On the other hand, *that* had been a play, *this* would be a film; a film would be less personal, less impertinent, there would be a director, a script editor, a cameraman and no doubt a number of creatively inputting producers, thus a shared responsibility, dispersed blame etc. So I re-read *The Invisible Woman*, parts of it twice, then put it back on the shelf, thinking, well, yes, and on the other hand, no. One night, very late, I took out a pad and a pencil and talked to myself in a hip-hop sort of fashion, conversational notes, really (see below) first about Dickens, and then about Dickens and Ellen Ternan, about them separately and about them together. The next morning I phoned Claire Tomalin, and we arranged to have lunch.

It was quite a long, jolly lunch, at the end of which it was agreed that I'd have a go at writing the film, and if by any chance a believable film producer came along with an offer of money but with a writer of his own she was to let me know, and if I felt I was making no progress, I would stand down, no hard feelings.

I've written lots and lots of films for television, lots and lots of them, and some have even won awards, but when I tried to write a film about Dickens and Ellen Ternan it was as if I'd had no previous experience, almost as if I'd never seen a film, had no idea of how a film flowed from one scene to another, how to see faces in close-up, where the camera should be – yes, that was the nub of it. I could imagine the characters and what they said to each other, but I couldn't imagine the camera. All my scenes took place in rooms with people sitting in a fixed relation to each other, occasionally getting up to walk closer or further away. I spent a year working against the grain – making up snappy new scenes, shortening and eliding old ones, cross-cutting from Ext. Garden, Gad's Hill to Int. Dressing Room, Theatre Royal – until one morning, as the yellow London dawn was breaking, I gave in to my dark and dangerous desire, and sent Claire Tomalin an email saying that actually I wasn't writing a film, I was writing a play. I hoped that was OK by her. She sent me a slightly perplexed email back, saying that it was, she supposed.

It took many months to get a first draft that I dared show anyone. Although I couldn't judge it myself, I had the feeling that it was alive but shapeless, which is better than shapely but dead – the disadvantage being that you can't bury it, *requiescat* and move on. In fact, a living piece of work is rather like a child in that it imposes obligations, demands attention, allows you to dream, and promises you nothing. I sent it to Simon Callow, who read it and agreed that there was a pulse. I did some more work, and sent it to Claire Tomalin, who thought so too. I did some more work and sent it to Peter Hall, who gave me further hope. Then I did some more work and then I did some more work and then I did some more work until I couldn't think of any more work to do, and then I did some more work.

Bernard Shaw said that writing a play was either easy or impossible. My play wasn't impossible, I'd been at it too long and spent too much of my best blood on it to allow it to be impossible. I reverted to my long-ago tactic of stealing up on it when it wasn't looking, and then batter, batter, batter, 'Come out you bastard, and fight!' etc., but of course I was nearly forty years on, and overweight and short of breath. I decided to give up violence in favour of cheating. I put what I thought to be my best draft on the computer, and then extracted from it drafts galore, sometimes attaching the top half of one draft to the bottom half of another, or a quarter on top of three-quarters, interminable desperate jugglings accomplished by jabbing the copy, cut, paste buttons – synthesised writing, I suppose you could call it. This is the great thing about the computer, for someone of my generation with my sort of temperament, that it gives you the illusion of work – you go to bed at five in the morning with squinty eyes, a befuddled head, and an unnatural but satisfied sense of having cut, copied and pasted yourself to oblivion, from which you will return to copy, paste and cut – what can this be but hard and complicated work? Even if you have the odd moment in which you suspect you've turned yourself into a technological Casaubon.

Eventually I bullied myself back to the typewriter, knowing that at least I would think before I wrote, and with luck, while I was writing. When the typewriter failed I went back to pads and pencil, and when they didn't help I had nothing left to try, really, except perhaps a quill pen on parchment, followed by flint on stone walls, followed by fingernails into flesh finally enraged beyond endurance by the sheer frustration of being me – a bad workman run out of tools to blame.

In desperation, really, I sent one of the last drafts to the usual trio – Callow, Hall and Tomalin – who replied in their usual encouraging terms, though I had a suspicion that they didn't see in it much difference from the one I'd sent them over a year before. My consolation was that they didn't say that they'd found it any worse, thus sustaining my belief that I hadn't yet beaten or strangled it to death. Nevertheless, I fell into a depressed sloth, and took to wondering why I hadn't taken up a different profession – followed my father, say, into pathology, and then remembered that he, too, was prone to bouts of depression, from spending too much time in the company of corpses, and of women not his wife. But then he was a full Scot, I only half a Scot, so for him the completely dead with lots of life on the side, for me a half-life – those sorts of thoughts, blaming and self-pitying in equal measure, in keeping with my idea of the spirit of the age.

So I was on my knees, my least favourite writing position, when through the ether came an email inviting me to write a play for BBC Radio Four. It was from Jane Morgan, whom I've known and liked for years, and who is a joy to work with, and who knows about cricket, even checking the county scores, as I do sometimes. Furthernore this would be our fifth play together. Oh, how I would love, I said, absolutely love, but alas! I had nothing in me, and on my computer and in a drawer only a large number of nearly finished stage plays about Charles Dickens and his mistress Ellen Ternan. Oh yes, she said, she knew Claire Tomalin's book, could I think of making a radio version? I sent her what I currently thought to be the three best drafts, and we arranged to meet to go through them in detail. We spent long afternoons on the radio play, I spent long nights on the stage play, and lo! in what seemed like no time we had the radio play, and I had three more drafts of the stage play, possibly four – a few hours on the computer could generate another six, ten before dawn, I could see myself back to where I had been, and from there only on and on until kindly Death – but before either prolixity or paralysis could set in I cast the three drafts aside, switched off the computer, and without once looking back, wrote what I knew to be the first and final draft of *Little Nell*.

So to adjust Bernard Shaw's dictum, one could say that writing a play is impossible until it's written. Of course, as Bernard Shaw also said, whether it's any good is a different matter.

THE NOTES

Of all great writers he's the one who makes the most palpable claim on our emotions, with so many ways of asserting his claim, so many voices and tones, savage, gentle, intimate, melodramatic, boisterous, lyrical, pastoral, comical, historical, hysterical, lachrymose, embarrassing – he never leaves you alone, in every paragraph he's there in front of you, with his hands on your shoulders, or beside you with his arm hooked under yours – and yet you haven't really the slightest idea, not really, of who he is –

One sees the faces, the expressions, the gestures of the characters, but one never, with the exception of Pip and the young David Copperfield, lives inside them, as one does with Tolstoy's, or shares the author's understanding of them, as one does with Jane Austen – for all the vividness and detail, they are actually mysterious. Where could they come from? Possibly an alternative universe, you can sometimes glimpse it, a surreal tavern, say, with inward-sloping walls and a dipping roof, at one askew table Squeers hobnobbing with Bounderby and Bagstock, at another Bucket consulting with Jaggers and Carker. Even in the great narrative passages, the openings of *Bleak House*, *Little Dorrit*, *Hard Times*, the descriptions of the river in *Our Mutual Friend*, you hear an impersonation of a narrator –

I'm looking at the picture of him in my study, not a very good one, it must be said, a water-colour done from a photograph, but it's recognisably him, at the end of his life – tired the face is, lined, much older than his years, rather posed and intense, something a bit fraudulent in the whole effect – a face without a childhood might be a way of putting it, no sense at all of evolution in it, no whiff of the blacking factory. And when you read contemporary accounts of him, of his brightness, his quickness, his merriment, so mercurial, so whimsical, so affectionate, on and on in such terms, you're left with the feeling that he's been encountered in a book, though one not written by himself – he would have made himself more particular, given us the necessary distortions to remember him by. Even people who disliked him somehow failed to see him – they write of his vulgarity, his dandyism and charlatanism, all the externals, and then conclude in a flurry of judgements and abstractions – although come to think of it that's not true of John Forster, his biography makes him seem real even though it's full of lies and omissions, and his Dickens, who has a long and eventually unhappy marriage and, of course, no extramarital sex life, still has a powerful sexuality – but then Forster knew him as only a heterosexual intimate, alert to competitive male impulses, could know him – and Forster had a touch of genius himself.

At one point in his life, towards the ghastly end of it, I suppose, Tolstoy had no time for fiction – fiction was lies, he thought – nevertheless he allowed *David Copperfield* on his bedroom bookshelf because it was a true book about childhood – and certainly the first half of it is the greatest novel ever written about childhood – and *Great Expectations*, probably the greatest about growing up, and I think, actually, the greatest novel in the English language. Or is *Little Dorrit* the greatest novel in the English language, or might it be *Bleak House* – and so suddenly one is gaping at the enormity of the achievement – how was it possible that a man could sustain a creative life at such a pitch? Balzac I suppose comes closest, I love Balzac and read him now more often than I read Dickens, but really not even *Cousin Bette*, say, put beside *Little Dorrit*, say – so when you're fretting away about who he was, you should keep in mind that ultimately who he was was the man who wrote that and that and that – ungraspable by a man like you, who has written only this and this and this – so perhaps the mystery is just the mystery of his overwhelming genius, your bafflement at being overwhelmed. On the other hand, just like a man like me, he had to live his other life, the life of daily needs in a daily self.

His daily needs in a daily self. How categorise the episodes of sexual lunacy during his twenties and thirties? His grotesque idealising of his dead sister-in-law, for instance, his dancing of the pretty Miss X into the sea at midnight, his creepy mesmeric experiments on young Mrs Y in Italy? Were these just expressions of his superabundant creativity, the mighty life-force spurting down eccentric subsidiary channels? Well, there were also the men-only trips to Paris with Wilkie Collins et al. – lots of fun there, I expect, but nothing for the daily needs, daily self –

Lots of critics claim that he couldn't do women – in my view he could do women, terrifying women at least, better than most – Miss Wade, Mrs Gamp, Mrs Joe, Mrs Skewton, Mrs Merdle, on and on the list – the ghastly joke about them is their sex – their ghastly flashes of sexuality – just think of Miss Mowcher, the 'id' as a garrulous dwarf.

Think too of David's crush on Steerforth, yes, but David's is a heterosexual's crush. In my view.

Sexual lunacy is probably not the right phrase, but I can't think what the right phrase is. Let's just say that his life from early puberty on was a frantic struggle not to 'come out' as a needy, predatory and mostly desperate heterosexual.

How could he not be desperate? All he had for his daily needs and daily self was poor old daily needy Catherine, whose obedient touch he must have come to hate, as he hated her clumsiness, and who gave him all those children to provide for.

He was possibly the most famous man in the world, and certainly the world's most famous family man. To have been caught betraying his wife would have turned him into a sort of Pecksniff of adultery.

So he stuck out his marriage from his early twenties to his mid-forties, all the while tortured by longings that he didn't dare satisfy – at least until at forty-five he seduced Ellen Ternan, an eighteen-year-old actress, who gave him, I hope, sexual freedom at last – though 'I hated his touch,' she is said to have said after his death, when she had become Mrs Robinson, the headmaster's wife.

He should have died in Ellen Ternan's arms, but didn't quite – so she had to smuggle his dying and paralysed body from their little home in Slough to his family home in Gad's Hill, then scuttle off while Georgina, mistress of his household and sister of his dismissed wife, set about organising a respectable death and a respectable version of it – how he'd worked all day in his study in the garden, gone out to post some letters, come back for dinner, begun to stumble, jumbled his speech, fallen sideways – actually I forget the details but they were along those lines, medically appropriate and socially becoming. Ellen was allowed a brief visit, either just before or just after the end, in her role as favourite goddaughter, I can't remember whether she was also allowed to the funeral in Westminster Abbey, I have an idea that she watched from behind a pillar – yes, of course, because that's where she was seen by the vicar, Benham, to whom she later confessed –

And then, well, she had to start life thirteen years behind, so to speak, thirteen unaccountable years to account for, thirteen years of domestic intimacy interrupted by regular and irregular separations, thirteen years of waitings, welcomings, partings. She saw him decline from an exuberant middle-aged man at the height of his powers to the morphine-and-brandy-dependent, gout-and-piles-ridden wreck of the last months while she went from a young woman in her prime to, by the reckonings of those days, a woman well past it. So when one says, 'The affair lasted thirteen years, just think!' one is in fact saying more than one can bear to think, when one tries to think some sort of content into just a few days of the thirteen years.

Let's try to think of them at the halfway stage, six and a half years into their life together, she in their front room, perhaps playing the piano, waiting for his footstep. Did her heart rise or did it sink when she heard it? And his heart, as he approached the door?

The evenings stretching before them possibly tender, domestic and charming as they sang duets. Or interminable and boring, a bit like 'A Game of Chess' in *The Waste Land*, but punctuated with sex. She hated his touch, don't forget. Or so she said.

He had ten children, wasn't it, by Catherine, if you include the two she lost, and in her subsequent marriage to the headmaster George Robinson she had two, the first when she was nearly forty – so in the course of thirteen years how did it happen that this productive man and this fertile woman failed to produce a child? Of course with hoops and crinoline and all that stuff it would have been hard to tell – And there were her long mysterious spells in France where he visited her occasionally.

Perhaps he dropped the babies off at the nearest orphanage, like Rousseau – much nicer to think that they practised contraception. What sort of contraception could be practised in the 1860s? I must look it up, or ask around.

So after his death, some years as Miss Ternan again, then marriage to George Robinson, and there she was, respectable Mrs Robinson, the headmaster's wife.

Mrs Robinson. Now there's a title.

She could account to her devoted husband George for some – say ten – of the missing years by simply knocking them off her age, the other three by lies about illness, convalesence in Italy, and so forth. Did George sense, in a befuddled male sort of way, that he had a wife not completely his? Something certainly happened that caused him to dwindle from cheerful, robust, responsible into withdrawn, depressed and useless – useless as a breadwinner, possibly useless as a husband and a father – useless at least for the son, Geoffrey –

The son, Geoffrey had speech difficulties, was it a lisp?

Geoffrey made a career in the army to please his mother, like Coriolanus, fought in the First War, and then retired from the army to run a secondhand bookshop in Slough, where, unknown to him, his mother had lived in sin with one of the world's most famous men. Quite a coincidence, unless he was directed there by some perverse homing instinct. Apart from a mildly unhappy marriage, he led a quiet life in his bookshop in Slough until, thanks to Benham the vicar, he came across gossipy bits in newspapers about Charles Dickens (now fifty years dead) and a young actress called Ellen Ternan (now nine years dead). He must have been first bewildered and then angry – it was preposterous, impossible, salacious, nonsensical, etc. – nothing could have been more innocent than his mother's childhood love of her famous godfather, she'd talked about it often to him, with joy and movingly, she'd read the novels aloud at bedtime. Besides, his mother had never been an actress, she would have mentioned it to him.

Geoffrey obtained an interview with Dickens's son Henry, a distinguished lawyer some thirty years older than himself. All we know about the interview is that after it Geoffrey cleared all the works of Dickens out of his house, divorced his wife, gave up the bookshop, then became his mother's son and went into acting.

He didn't make much of a fist of it, from the little that's known, but there are records of appearances in minor parts in theatres around the Tottenham Court Road area.

Little Nell was first broadcast on BBC Radio 4 on
16 December 2006, produced by Pier Productions, with
the following cast:

Sir Henry Dickens Philip Voss
Geoffrey Robinson Crispin Redman
Ellen Ternan Monica Dolan
Charles Dickens Michael Pennington
Jane Maria Miles
George Wharton Robinson Nicholas Boulton
Rev Benham Nicholas Le Prevost

Directed by Jane Morgan
Technical Presentation Roy Fraser
Production Manager Jane Ellison
Pianist Charlotte Brennand

Characters

Henry
Geoffrey

Dick
Nelly
Jane
George
Benham
Aldersley
Clara
Crayford

LITTLE NELL

Lights up on the stage of the Free Trade Hall, Manchester. Saturday 22 August 1857.

The last moments of the play The Frozen Deep *by Wilkie Collins.*

The scene takes place at the back of a cave in the Arctic regions. Wardour, played by Charles Dickens (Dick), is stretched out centre stage. He is dying. Aldersley is lying half propped up, some distance from him. Clara is kneeling by him. Crayford is standing to the side, watching. Lucy, played by Ellen Ternan (Nelly) is standing near Wardour.

Crayford Wardour, look at me! Look at your old friend!

Wardour (*vacantly*) My friend? Yes, yes, yes – He looks kindly at me – he looks like a friend. My eyes are dim, friend – my mind is dull – I have lost all memories but the memory of her. Dead thoughts – all dead thoughts but that one! And yet, he looks kindly? Why has his face gone down with the wreck of all the rest? Hark ye, friend? Never let Frank know it! There was a time when the fiend within me hungered for his life.

Crayford Hush! Hush!

Wardour I took him away alone – away with me over the waste of snow – he on one side, and the tempter on the other, and I between them, marching, till the night fell and the campfire was all aflame. If you can't kill him, leave him, leave him when he sleeps, the tempter whispered me – leave him when he sleeps! I set him his

3

place to sleep in apart; but he crept between the Devil and me, and nestled his head on my breast, and slept here. Leave him! Leave him! the voice whispered. Lay him down in the snow and leave him! Love him, the lad's voice answered, moaning and murmuring, here, in his sleep – Love him, Clara, for helping me! Love him for my sake! I heard the night wind come up in the silence from the great deep. It bore past me the groanings of the icebergs at sea, floating, floating past! – And the wicked voice floated away with it – away, away, away for ever! Love him, Clara, for helping me! No wind could float that away! Love him, Clara – (*His voice dies away and his head sinks.*)

Aldersley Help me up! I must go to him! Clara, come with me. (*Approaches Wardour.*) Wardour! Oh, help Wardour! Clara, speak to him!

Clara Richard!

No answer.

Aldersley Richard!

Wardour Ah, poor Frank! I didn't forget you, Frank, when I came here to beg. I remembered you, lying down outside in the shadow of the rocks. I saved your share of food and drink. Too weak to get at it now! A little rest, Frank! I shall soon be strong enough to carry you down to the ship!

Aldersley Get something to strengthen him, for God's sake! Oh, men! Men! I should never have been here but for him! He has given all his strength to my weakness; and now, see how strong I am, and how weak he is! Clara! I held by his arm all over the ice and snow. His hand dragged me from the drowning men when we were wrecked. He kept watch when I was senseless in the open boat. Speak to him, Clara – speak to him again!

4

Clara Richard, dear Richard, look at your old playmate! Have you forgotten me?

Music: 'River, River', merging at 'Kiss me before I die!' into 'Those Evening Bells', which lasts until the curtain has fallen.

Wardour Forgotten you?

He lays his hand on Aldersley's head.

Should I have been strong enough to save him, if I could have forgotten you? Stay! Someone was here and spoke to me just now. Ah! Crayford! I recollect now. (*Embracing him.*) Dear Crayford! Come nearer! My mind clears, but my eyes grow dim. You will remember me kindly for Frank's sake? Poor Frank! Why does he hide his face? Is he crying? Nearer, Clara – I want to look my last at you! My sister, Clara! (*She falls on him, sobbing.*) Kiss me, sister, kiss me before I die!

Lucy comes forward, kneels beside Clara, stroking her head.

Lights slightly down to create a tableau: Lucy, Clara and the dying Wardour the main grouping.

Lights up on the office of Sir Henry Dickens, 1922.

Henry (*scanning a letter*) Hah! We'll see. (*He pushes down button on intercom.*) You can send Mr Robinson in now. (*Puts the letter in front on him.*)

There is a knock on the door.

Come in. (*He stands.*)

Geoffrey enters. He is in his forties, stiff and shy, with a military bearing, He has an occasional stutter, not always specified in the text.

Sorry to have kept you waiting, Mr Robinson. I asked my secretary to give you a cup of tea – did he do that?

Geoffrey Yes. Th—

Henry Well, how can I help you, sir?

Geoffrey has a little trouble speaking.

In your letter – (*Picking up letter.*) – you mention a legacy.

Geoffrey It's a confidential matter.

Henry Of course it is. And I am a lawyer. That's why you're here.

Geoffrey A family matter.

Henry Yes, sir. It's likely to be. Most matters discussed in this office are family matters.

Geoffrey (*after a pause, apologetically*) I meant your family. We are connected, you see. In a sense connected.

Henry 'In a sense connected.' (*Nods.*) In other words, you are a claimant. I had the feeling the instant I saw the envelope. It had the look of a claimant's envelope. (*Gets up, opens the door.*) Before you go, Mr Robinson, I will give you some professional advice, without charge. Your best course is to end your adventure with this interview. Over the years I've become used to half-brothers, half-sisters, quarter-grandsons – (*Laughs.*) – turning up with doctored documents and fraudulent demands. Several have been lucky not to have ended up in gaol. All of them wasted their time and their money – far more of the latter than they could afford. Only my fellow lawyers benefited. Now please – (*Gestures towards door.*)

Geoffrey doesn't move.

I can have an officer in two minutes.

Geoffrey I'm not here for money. I want information.

Henry Information about what?

Geoffrey My – my – mm – mother.

Henry Your mother? Who was your – Robinson? Wharton Robinson?

Geoffrey My father. My mother was Ellen Ternan before she married.

Henry Ellen – Nelly. Of course. Nelly Ternan. Why didn't you make your identity clear in your letter?

Geoffrey I wasn't sure you would see me. You would take me for – (*Gestures.*) – a claimant.

Henry And you aren't? Well, now I look at you properly – (*Doing so.*) I can see. My apologies. May we start again?

He comes around, offers hand. They shake hands.

Good. Well that's that, then. Let's make ourselves – (*Gestures to chair.*) May I ask you about yourself? You were in the war, I think?

Geoffrey Yes.

Henry Bad business. Bloody and bad. But I don't need to tell you that.

Geoffrey No.

Henry Where did you fight?

Geoffrey Flanders. Mons. Afterwards I was sent to Persia. Azerbaijan.

Henry To keep an eye on the Bolsheviks, eh?

Geoffrey nods.

So you must be a bit of a linguist. Russian at least?

Geoffrey Learnt it from my aunt.

Henry That would be Florence.

Geoffrey No, Maria. Aunt Maria. She travelled to Russia and –

Henry Oh yes, of course. Maria the traveller and artist. Florence, Fanny, was the novelist. They were remarkable women, your aunts. Adventurous. Ahead of their time. New women –

Geoffrey Yes.

Henry I was sorry to hear of their deaths. And of your mother's, of course. My father was very fond of your mother, as I expect you know.

Geoffrey She was very proud of the connection.

Henry And what do you do now, may I ask?

Geoffrey I keep a secondhand bookshop. In Slough.

Henry Ah. Some tranquillity. After the horrors.

Geoffrey Horrors?

Henry Of the war.

Geoffrey Oh. Oh yes. The war.

There is a pause.

Henry Well then, well then. You said you wanted information. How can I help?

Geoffrey After my mother's death I found a box. It contained a number of things – items – that – that – there was a poster of a play. This –

8

He takes it out of his briefcase and hands it to Henry.

Henry (*taking it*) *The Frozen Deep*! Good Heavens! (*Involuntary smile of recognition.*) I was in it. Well, not in it, but around the edges, an extra. All of us had parts. The children, that is – (*Stops.*) But of course your mother's name caught your eye?

Geoffrey It was an amateur production, was it?

Henry Yes. Well, no. Half and half, so to speak. You see, in those days when my father got up a production – especially a successful one, like *The Frozen Deep* – he and his friends played the men's parts, but it wasn't thought becoming for women to appear before a paying audience so their parts were played by professional actresses. So your mother and her two sisters – your aunts, Maria and Fanny – and their mother too, your grandmother – the whole family, in fact – all actresses, and all in *The Frozen Deep*. Actually, I'm not sure about Fanny – but your grandmother certainly, she played –

Geoffrey She was a professional actress then?

Henry Your grandmother?

Geoffrey My mother.

Henry Yes. She was.

Geoffrey She was born in 1850. Or so she said.

Henry 1850?

Geoffrey *The Frozen Deep* was performed in Manchester on the evening of August 22nd 1857.

Henry (*looks down at the poster*) So it was. Good heavens, that's what? Sixty-five years ago. Sixty-five years! Good heavens!

9

The cast of The Frozen Deep *take their bows to ghostly applause and cheering.*

Geoffrey So according to her account, my mother would have been seven years old when she played the part of a young woman in *The Frozen Deep*.

Henry Ah. I see. Yes. (*Laughs.*) Well, needless to say, she wasn't seven. She was – at least seventeen. Yes, seventeen would be about right. (*Little pause.*) So she told you she was born in '50? Well, you know how women can be about their age, when they're past a certain age. They make subtractions, forgetting that they're likely to create confusion later about earlier periods in their lives.

Geoffrey Is that when they met, then? During *The Frozen Deep* in Manchester?

Henry Who?

Geoffrey My mother and your father?

Cast exits, Dick holding Nelly's and Maria's hands.

Henry Oh. Yes. I believe so. It seems to me rather odd, Mr Robinson, may I say? That you've come to me to acquire information about your own – own family –

Geoffrey My whole world has become very odd, Sir Henry. To discover that my mother had another life – a past quite unlike the one she used to describe to me.

Henry Well, there's a likely explanation. In her days, you know, actresses weren't quite – as – as they are now. She married a schoolteacher, did she not? Your father – Wharton Robinson – was a Headmaster?

Geoffrey nods.

She probably felt it was wiser, from the point of view of the parents, the governors – and she wouldn't have

wanted to burden her child with the responsibility of –
(*Gestures.*) – concealment.

Geoffrey It wasn't just concealment. She lied outright.
She said that Charles Dickens died when she was a child.

Henry Once she'd deducted ten years from her age, she
had no choice but to make everything fit.

There is a pause.

May I ask, in what terms exactly did your mother describe
her relationship to my father?

Geoffrey She used to tell me that he appointed himself
unofficial uncle to the family. And godfather, a sort of
godfather, to her. She loved to describe a particular
afternoon when he took them all on an outing to
Doncaster. The sun was shining, they had such a picnic,
with such laughter and jollity – he did conjuring tricks,
she sat on his knee as he told stories, they sang songs
and at the end of it he made his great pronouncement –
that from that day forth he was to be known as Uncle
to each and every one of the Ternan ladies, with special
godfatherly responsibilities for the youngest of them.

Henry The whole family was there, mother and three
daughters?

*Lights half up on a park in Doncaster, August 1857.
Afternoon.*

*Nelly (seventeen) and Charles Dickens (forty-five) are
walking arm in arm. Dick is holding Nelly's arm in a
correct, gentlemanly fashion.*

Geoffrey She could remember their clothes and the
hats they wore. The contents of the enormous picnic

hamper he'd brought from London . . . She would
always laugh when she remembered it, and cry a little
before she'd finished telling me. It was the happiest day
of her childhood, because her sisters and mother were
so happy too.

Lights fully up on Dick and Nelly.

Dick I'm so sorry that your dear mother and Maria and
Fanny couldn't be with us this afternoon, of all afternoons.
Such a beautiful one.

Nelly Yes, I hate to think of them in that draughty old
theatre. But then they're so pleased to have the parts.
(*Little pause.*) We're grateful to you for recommending
them.

Dick I'm always pleased to be of service. To you. And
to your family. I have given you nothing that you don't
deserve. You have such hard lives.

Nelly Do we?

Dick I know – I know something of what it's like for
you. The conditions which you have to endure. The little
house in Islington.

Nelly It's a perfect little house. We love it.

Dick Park Cottage, is it not?

Nelly Yes. Park Cottage. (*Little pause.*) You've seen it,
then?

Dick Yes. I followed you home last Wednesday. The
three of you. I kept you in my sights. All the way from
the stage door of the theatre to Park Cottage, to make
sure you got home safely. And then I peeped once, only
once and very quickly, through the window.

Nelly And what did you see?

12

Dick I saw a devoted mother and her three devoted daughters.

Nelly Yes, but what did you see, what were we doing? What were we doing, what were you looking at us doing? Oh, I can't bear it to think of anyone, of you above all, looking at us.

Dick You were doing the most ordinary things, that was the charm of you. Fanny was helping Maria off with her coat, and behind them your mother had gone to the kitchen. She was slicing bread.

There is a pause.

Nelly And I? What was I doing?

Dick Yes. What were you doing?

Nelly I was coming down the stairs. And I had a feeling – a feeling of being looked at. Through the window.

Dick You saw me, then? Yes. Your smile – (*Looks at her, almost touches her on the mouth.*) – that I know, I know as if I've known it all my life. But how can that be, how can that be, when we've had so little time together. Tell me, Nelly, my – my little Nell. May I call you that?

Nelly But she died, your Little Nell. I shall never forget Ma reading it out to us when we were little. I cried for her, we all cried, Maria and Fanny, and Ma too, even when we knew it almost by heart we still hoped that it would end differently this time, that you'd save her, hoped and prayed that you'd save her, and you never did, not once – oh, it was very hard to forgive you.

Dick It was the most terrible thing I ever did. I cried, too, when I knew it had to be done. But you – you have undone it, you see. Here you are. Alive. Alive again. Out of my story and into my life. And so – so very alive.

Nelly How do I know you won't kill me again?

Dick Will you trust me?

Nelly With my life, you mean?

Dick (*after a pause*) Yes. Yes, I believe I do mean that. With my life.

Nelly What would I have to do?

Dick Have to do? Why would you have to do anything, but be? Be. My Nell.

Nelly And what would you be to me?

Dick What would you have me be?

Nelly I don't know. I don't know what is – (*Hesitates.*)

Dick What is?

Nelly Right.

Dick Ah. Yes. Well, would it be right to be your friend? Your friend and protector? A godfather to you? Or an uncle?

Nelly My godfather? Oh!

Dick You like that, then?

Nelly I haven't got a godfather. Or an uncle, even.

Dick Then I shall be both. Both your uncle and your godfather.

Nelly Uncle would be better. Because I could give you a name, couldn't I? I couldn't call you Godfather Charles, could I, but I could call you –

Dick Uncle Charles.

Nelly Uncle Charles. Yes. May I?

14

Dick You may. And may I – may I celebrate the sudden appearance in the world of a fully formed, long established – how long has it been, oh, at least forty-five seconds, now forty-six, seven seconds, which in my soul feels like the longest, deepest, truest lastingest relationship, the relationship avuncular, the relationship protective and the relationship godfatherly, to which you are also entitled. Godly – holy, a holy and most sacred attachment, may I, my dear girl, oh my dear Little Nell, celebrate it with a holy and sacred, avuncular and most godfatherly kiss. (*Kisses her gently on the forehead.*) And how would you like to celebrate it? (*Holding her by the shoulders.*) What will you ask?

Nelly Oh – oh, there's nothing – nothing more I could want. Thank you. Thank you –

Dick You can say it. Our name for me.

Nelly Uncle Charles.

Dick It doesn't sound quite right, does it, when it's said. Uncle Charles. Its breeches are very starched, it has a tight waistcoat, because of a tight, round, important stomach, and a waxy moustache and a little spade of a beard that could jab through all the softness and roundness and sweetness of things. No, Uncle Charles isn't the man we took him to be.

Nelly There's Uncle Charlie.

Dick Uncle Charlie goes to the races, loses his wife's money, gets drunk, fails to come home, falls into gutters – goes to Paris for his pleasures.

Nelly Well – (*Laughs.*)

Dick What? What?

Nelly I quite like the sound of him.

Dick So do I.

Nelly I should love to go to Paris.

Dick And you shall. But not with Uncle Charlie. I can see him, can't you, swaggering his way along the boulevards, one arm tucked under yours – (*Tucks his arm under Nelly's.*) – as jaunty as a dancing master, and behind the two of you trots poor old Uncle Charles, from Gad's Hill, worrying in his pockets whether he's enough cash on him to pay for the two of you, your escapades – and then there'll be dancing, yes. Uncle Charlie will take you to a dancing, and when he arises from the table, offers you his hand, with a perfect little bow, leads you onto the floor. (*Does this.*) Uncle Charles sits with a fixed smile on his face, poor old thing, his foot tapping out of time to the music, because it's at odds with the music in his heart, and you'll look at me with such pity as you sweep by. Indeed, you'll pause, indeed you will, and you'll say, 'Oh, Uncle Charles, why don't you go back to the hotel and rest, Uncle Charlie will look after me –'

He is sweeping her about, as if to music.

Nelly Oh, I won't, indeed I won't.

Dick What will you say?

Nelly I'll say – I'll say – 'Now that's enough, Uncle Charlie, quite enough of you and your impertinences! I'm out with my nunky – and it's time he took me home, took me home to – to – to the hotel. He has work to do. He is a great man with great work to do, and we have no time to waste with wastrels like you! (*Taking Dick's arm.*) So you stay here, Uncle Charlie – and settle the bill, if you please!'

She walks properly along with Dick, but clinging to his arm.

Dick (*stopping*) So it's to be Nunky, then?

Nelly Nunky. Well, if I may – if you think it suitable –

Dick What are you looking at?

Nelly Your face.

Dick And what do you see?

Nelly Your eyes.

Dick Ah, then you see yourself. Because they're full of you. They can see nothing else. Oh, but my beard! You've never seen me without it, have you, Little Nell? Well, I only grew it for the play. I'll shave it first thing tomorrow morning. No. Tonight. As soon as I have my razor in my hand I'll make myself a clean and moral chin again.

Nelly No no! I love it – love it as it is!

Dick Love it? Do you? Then I promise – a vow, I make a solemn vow that this beard will only perish at your command.

Nelly Never!

  She puts a hand out to touch it, but doesn't.

Dick Don't be shy of it! Are you shy of it?

Nelly Yes.

Dick Why? Why are you?

Nelly Because it belongs to you. It is you.

Dick Not if you want it. If you want it, it shall belong to you. Take it and see. (*Juts his chin at her.*)

Nelly (*puts her hand on the beard, tugs it gently*) It won't let me.

Dick Ah well, you can't have him by force, you have to coax him off.

Nelly (*strokes the beard, runs her fingers through it*) Oh, it's so soft, so soft, like a baby's beard – oh – oh – so delicate and soft and lovely. (*Pulls it.*) But it's still yours.

Dick It is almost yours. You almost have it.

Nelly What must I do?

Dick There's something you must do.

Nelly But what?

Dick Only you can know. He's at your mercy.

Nelly Perhaps I should bite him. Would he mind if I bit him?

Dick Let us find out.

Nelly bites Dick's beard. Then nibbles at it, then nibbles around it. Then looks into his face.

Nelly Is he mine now?

Dick No. He still seems to be mine. He is clinging to me. He wants – he wants an exchange, little Nell.

Nelly What are we to do, then? As I haven't a beard for you to eat, Nunky.

Dick Nell, my dearest little creature, with brightest eyes and glowing cheeks and hair a-tumble, tumble, and loveliest, sweetest self within, without, my mouse of a Nelly Nell Nell, there's not a part of you I don't long to eat, to eat. Ah Nell – and full pink lips, did I specify my little Nell mouse's full pink lips, I long to eat and eat –

He kisses her gently on the lips, and then more and more devouringly, then stops, walks away a few steps.

There is a pause.

18

Nelly What is it, Nunky, what is it?

Dick Nunky – yes, well, now that I'm a nunky – Today we are in Doncaster, no, we are not in Doncaster, we're in our own little paradise that the rest of the world calls Doncaster, but tomorrow we – I – am back in London, in a nunkly world, and in a nunkly world there are nunkly difficulties. And responsibilities. Nunkly responsibilities. Your sisters, for instance. Fanny says she wants to stop acting and become a singer. A trained singer. She is talented, she has a lovely voice, it deserves the best of teachers, which are to be found, I understand, in Italy.

Nelly Fanny – go to Italy? But all by herself, without Mama and me, how will she manage?

Dick Your mama will go with her.

Nelly Oh. But Maria –

Dick Maria will stay with you for a while. Until we find a little house – no, not a little house, like Park Cottage, but a house of a size for happiness. It will be a house with large windows, and outside the air will be clean and healthy, there will be pleasant walks, and a piano – we shall have a piano, and we shall sing duets together by the hearth and we shall be as perfect and compact and neat and harmonious a little family as the world has never before seen or read about.

Nelly (*after a pause*) But how can we be like that – when you already have a family? You are married, Nunky.

Dick Never! Never, never married! Not in my heart, not in my soul – married only in form and in law, a marriage I long ago annulled in my spirit, before it could annul my spirit. My wife is – my wife was – no, I will not speak of her, it would be wrong to speak of her at a moment like this, here, here and now, Mouse, at the beginning of my life. Ours will be the first marriage of my heart and soul, my first and only true marriage. Come, my little Nell. Come.

He goes to her, holds out his arms. Nelly creeps into them.

Take my beard and pull – pull the devil out of it! It is yours now, yours, only yours.

Nelly puts her hand on his beard.

Pull it hard, pull it hard – it's the devil, don't forget!

Nelly pulls it firmly, then savagely. Dick lets out a cry, pulls her to him, kisses her passionately.

My dearest – my dearest – oh, my dearest –

He pulls her to the ground.

Sir Henry's office.

Henry Uncle and godfather – that is very like my father. He was uncle and godfather to quite a few, over the years – it made it easier for them to accept his help.

Geoffrey But why should she pretend that she was a child instead of a young woman?

Henry Well, as I've already suggested – from a quite common sort of female vanity. And – as I think I've also said – to escape from her theatrical past. For your father's sake, as a headmaster. (*Pause.*) And of course she was probably anxious to dispel any gossip and rumours – there are always so many after the death of a great man. And if we're not careful they take root, they grow, become accepted. For instance, my own aunt, Georgina, my mother's sister, who looked after the family when my mother left the household, was suspected of being rather more to my father than very dear friend and housekeeper. (*Gestures dismissively.*) My father knew the sort of thing that was going the rounds, he treated it with contempt, needless to say. And there's been other talk, only quite recently, I believe, snippets and fragments of nonsense, nasty nonsense, there always has been, always, but now especially in these times we live in, these salacious and unfeeling times –

Geoffrey (*takes a newspaper out of his briefcase, hands it to Henry*) Like this, you mean?

Henry Oh that, yes. (*Glancing down.*) Poor old Wright. Thomas Wright. Yes. Precisely the sort of thing I mean.

Geoffrey He names my mother. He says he's writing a book –

Henry He's been writing it for decades. I doubt he'll ever publish it. And if he does –

Geoffrey If he does?

Henry His assertions are wild, unsubstantiated. By his own admission, it's thirty-five years since he heard the story, and his only source the gossip of that wretched clergyman, Benham, and he is long dead. Wright's book, if anyone dares publish it, will be received with contempt. Good heavens yes! Contempt!

There is a long pause.

Geoffrey Sir Henry – (*Hesitates, gets up.*) You've been most helpful, thank you.

Henry I'm only too happy to have been of service. Again my apologies for my initial misunderstanding – and as for your mother's little rearranging of history – well, women, you know, they have their secrets. As long as no real harm is done.

Getting up, he holds out his hand.

Geoffrey (*taking hand*) Sir Henry – um – um – (*He stammers something.*)

Henry Mmmm?

Geoffrey Was she – was my mother in fact – was she your father's mistress?

They are standing, holding hands.

Lights up on Dick and Nelly, some moments after we last saw them in Doncaster. She is on the ground, crouched slightly, as if in shock, her clothes in disarray. Dick is standing some distance from her, looking away from her, as if also in shock.

Dick (*going to Nelly*) Nell. Little Nell.

Nelly looks at him.

Don't be unhappy, Little Nell.

Nelly (*in a whisper*) I'm not unhappy, Nunky. I've never been so happy – so happy –

Dick (*putting coat around her*) You will be more happy. More and more happy. All the happiness that is mine to give, I shall give.

Nelly And all the happiness that is mine I shall give. I shall try so hard to be worthy of you. Worthy –

Dick Mouse. My mouse. But you are crying!

Nelly It's only because I hurt a little. Only a little, a very little.

Dick Oh. Oh yes, of course. Poor mouse. Poor little mouse, here, I have a – brought a –

He reaches in the jacket pocket of his coat, takes out a neatly folded towel, and hands it to Nelly.

Nelly Thank you. (*Dabs her eyes with it.*)

Dick It's a towel. I thought you might need a – Poor mouse. Poor little mouse –

He goes to her, gives her his hand. She takes it. He makes to raise her to her feet, instead kneels, taking her hand.

We're going to conquer the future, we are, with all the power of our hope. There will be no pain, no more pain.

He turns her hand over and looks into it.

I see it in your palm. Did you know I can read palms and tell the future? And in our future there is only happiness. You'll see, my mouse. You'll see.

Henry's office. Henry and Geoffrey are still holding hands.

Henry (*releasing hand*) His mistress!

Geoffrey nods his head.

I was hoping you wouldn't ask me directly. The lawyer in me, I suppose. So yes. Yes, I am afraid she was.

Geoffrey waits.

May I offer you some – I have some whisky.

Geoffrey Thank you. (*Sits down.*)

Henry goes to a cupboard, pours two glasses of whisky and brings glass and soda siphon to Geoffrey.

Henry Soda?

Geoffrey Thank you.

Henry squirts.

Thank you.

There is a pause.

Did it start when she was seventeen, then?

Henry I believe so, yes.

Geoffrey And he was – how old would he have been?

Henry Forty-five.

Geoffrey And for how long –?

Henry Until the day he died.

Geoffrey (*nods*) Until the day he died. (*Little pause.*) And that was in – Excuse me, I should know, of course. I expect I do, if I think –

Henry Thursday the 9th of June 1870.

Geoffrey I see. I see, I see. I see. (*Little pause.*) For thirteen years, then. Thirteen years. (*Looks at him, realising.*) So you must have known my mother, then?

Henry Yes.

Geoffrey (*after a pause*) What did you feel? About her and your father?

Henry She was – everything my father wanted.

24

Geoffrey Was she? Everything? A young woman – almost still a girl – and a man of his age, with the greatest success and fame. Everything he wanted?

Henry Oh, I know what you must be thinking. And of course that came into it. Naturally. But there was far more to it. In many respects it was like a marriage. They were even quite sedate. At least, they did the things together that settled and established couples do – for instance, they liked nothing better than to stay at home of an evening and sing duets. For hours and hours. They were in harmony, you see.

Sitting room in Slough. Summer 1862. Piano over. Dick and Nelly singing a duet.

Dick (*moved*) Oh, Mouse, it's cruel to have us sing that one, it always makes me weep.

Nelly No, it's only fair, because you make other people weep all the time, with your writing.

Dick (*takes out handkerchief, sits down*) Well then, let the tears be on you, you must mop them up.

He pats his knee. Nelly sits down on his knee, takes his handkerchief, wipes his eyes.

Nelly There.

She takes his handkerchief, puts it back in his pocket.

Dick Now I can see again. And what a heavenly sight.

He kisses her on the neck, on the cheek, on the forehead. Nelly scrambles off his knee as Jane enters, carrying a tray on which is port and a glass.

Ah! And here's our Jane.

Jane Yes, sir. (*Putting tray down.*)

Dick And how is your hand?

Jane I don't know, sir, quite well I think.

Dick Shall I have a look? (*Holding out his hand.*)

Jane gives him her hand, not eagerly. Dick starts to examine it.

Jane (*looks at Nelly, suddenly takes it away*) Oh, excuse me, sir – I'd rather not.

Dick Ah. Why not?

Jane makes to say something, doesn't. Lowers her head.

Nelly Perhaps because you keep promising her a husband.

Dick And a very handsome one. But I've never promised him immediately – only in the distant future.

Nelly But perhaps she doesn't want one at all.

Dick What, ever?

Jane (*shakes her head*) I'm quite happy where I am – I don't want anything else, if that's all right. (*Looks at Nelly.*) And I don't think I – I don't really want to know my fortune until it's on me, if – if –

She curtsies and runs out of room.

Dick Well. (*Laughs.*) Well, yes, of course she's right. We're better off blind. Sensible girl.

Nelly pours a glass of port and brings it to him.

Thank you, Mouse.

He takes the glass, then takes Nelly's hand, stares into it and raises it to his lips, kissing the palm.

And thank you, thank you.

Nelly What for?

Dick For being my mouse.

Nelly I sometimes wonder who knows –

Dick Knows what?

Nelly That I am your mouse.

Dick (*shocked*) Well, no one, of course.

Nelly Well then, how do you refer to me, when you're talking to your friends, for instance? Like Wilkie?

Dick I speak of you with – with respect and admiration, and love, of course – how else would I speak of you?

Nelly But how do you refer to me?

Dick It depends on the circumstances.

Nelly You mean you never refer to me?

Dick Everybody who knows me knows that I have a cherished young friend – a sort of niece or goddaughter – who is the daughter of my widowed friend Mrs Fanny Ternan. So of course I call you Miss Ternan or Nelly, depending on – on who it is I am speaking of you to.

Nelly Much easier than with Georgina, then?

Dick Georgina – what do you mean?

Nelly You can't give her a title so nobody really knows who she is.

Dick Everybody knows who she is. She is my sister-in-law.

Nelly But your wife has been sent to live somewhere else. Georgina, who is her sister, dwells in your house at Gad's Hill and cares for your children.

Dick (*laughing in spite of himself*) Dwells?

Nelly (*nodding*) Dwells. She dwells there. In Gad's Hill.

Dick Now come, Nell, come, come – why are we talking about this? You know the situation perfectly well. We've discussed it often enough –

Nelly But I still don't understand it, Nunky. You say she wasn't worthy of you and was bad for the children and probably mad, but still, there she is, called Mrs Charles Dickens – so shouldn't poor Georgina have some title to show that she's something more than just Miss Hogarth, your sister-in-law? She's your housekeeper and she looks after your children, and when you're at home, at your home in Gad's Hill, she does all those wifely things for you – though of course none of the things I do for you, but then I don't have a title to go around with either, do I? Except a false one, here in Peckham or when we're travelling together – when I'm wife to Mr Terdle, Teddle, Tiddle, Twaddle, depending on what name you're giving yourself –

Dick Come here, come back here, Mouse – (*Patting the arm of chair.*) – so I can answer you properly, you're whirling about so much.

Nelly I have been mainly quite still.

Dick Well, your words have been whirling about me – Come.

Nelly Very well. (*Sitting away from him.*) I'll listen.

Dick And what would you like to hear?

Nelly Whose fault it is that I have to be a false Mrs, to go with false names like Terdle, Nerdle, Twaddle and Woo – whose fault, Nunky?

Dick Whose fault? It is nobody's fault, my little Nell. Or rather, it is the world's fault. Do you wish you'd lived another life, then?

Nelly What other life was there for me? Once you'd come into it?

Dick You could have remained an actress, I suppose. And I'm sure many men would have fallen in love with you.

Nelly And would they have given me their name?

Dick The lucky one would have been able to give you his name. And I wouldn't have had my Little Nell.

Nelly And then what would you have done? What would have happened to you, if I'd stayed on the stage until someone else had swept me off it, into a respectable and doting marriage? Like Little Dorrit and her Arthur, going down the years to their happiness. What would you have done, if you'd seen me going down the years with Arthur somebody-or-other to a modest life of usefulness and happiness?

Dick I would have written myself into an early grave.

Nelly Oh. Died of a broken heart, you mean?

Dick Yes. I believe I would.

Nelly And if you'd never met me?

Dick Died of an empty heart.

Nelly Your heart could never be empty. It's full of love.

Dick But I'd have had no one to give it to. (*Puts his arm around her waist.*) Nell, my dearest, cleverest Little Nell –

Nelly (*interrupting*) No, no more, Nunky. I don't want you to say any more, or I shall – I shall – (*Puts her hand* *on his cheek.*) Do you remember when I used to rummage through your beard? Like this. (*Puts her fingers into his beard, pulling it gently.*) It was silky then. Silkier than my hair. (*Little pause.*) You are the world to me, Nunky. And yet it is the world's fault that I can never be a wife to you. So you say. I say it is the beard's fault. (*Pulls his beard.*) Naughty world. Naughty beard. Which is it?

She leans over, kisses him on the lips. He stands, pulls her to him. They kiss tenderly and sexually.

Office of SIr Henry.

Henry I realise that it might be difficult for you – to think that they achieved a, um – a happiness together under such circumstances.

Geoffrey Well, it would be a poor son who wished his mother ill in any situation she found herself in.

Henry That's very finely said, if I may say.

Geoffrey I'm having to get used to a great deal of – of new information. Rather quickly.

Henry Of course. Although clearly you had suspicions, more than suspicions, when you came here. In fact, it's why you came here.

Geoffrey I had – dread, sir. Dread. But I had some hope too – that it had been a romance – an innocent and unfulfilled romance. In his novels, after all, there is never even a hint – His fallen woman are lost, lost, and his good women are virtuous – There are no adulteries, as far as I remember.

Henry No. No adulteries. Although it has often been noticed that the young women in his later novels have a

30

vitality and a charm and sometimes behave somewhat inappropriately. Bella, in *Our Mutual Friend*, for instance. But in the end they turn out to be – as you say – virtuous.

Geoffrey She read them to me, you know, all the novels. My own favourite was *Great Expectations*.

Henry Mine too, I think. But not his. His was *David Copperfield*, his favourite child. (*Little pause.*) I became Pip for days on end.

Geoffrey Yes.

Henry He never read them out to me, though. Except when he read them publicly, and I was in the audience.

Geoffrey Ah. A case of the cobbler's son.

Henry Mmm? Oh, yes, I see. Not being shod. (*Laughs.*)

   There is a pause.

Geoffrey (*abruptly*) You must have hated her. You and the rest of your family. Hated her.

Henry Our lives changed because of her. Our mother suffered. He told us she was mad, you know. He told us that she didn't love us, had never loved us, was incapable of love. She was so bewildered, so hurt, so lost and unhappy. And we could see what your mother was, that our mother wasn't. Not simply young, but quick, lively, intelligent. And growing. Growing. Mama never kept pace with him. He always made her feel that. And of course I understand so much better now that he made her worse than she was – more incapable, more clumsy, more stupid, more helpless. Nelly, on the other hand – your mother – (*Little pause.*) We didn't hate her. We liked her. Yes. Even Georgina liked her. They got on.

Geoffrey Well, that's, that's – good to know. That she was popular with your family. I'm sorry about your mother, though. I apologise.

31

Henry I don't think – I don't think there's anything you need apologise for.

Geoffrey No, no, I know, I don't know why I did – I think I suddenly felt responsible. Ridiculous, of course – as if caught in a web. A web.

Henry May I –? (*Getting up, bringing whisky over.*)

Geoffrey Oh well, thank you, just a drop. I don't usually – at this time of day – needless to say.

Henry Oh, it's not the time of day that matters, it's the circumstance. A circumstance can happen at any time of the day.

He pours him a decent amount, and then for himself.

Are you married, by the way? May I ask?

Geoffrey No. That is, I am – I was – we are separated at the moment.

Henry No children, then?

Geoffrey No. My wife was keen but I felt that after such a war – It was difficult to think of bringing children into a world where such wars could happen.

Henry But you were a professional soldier? Before the war –

Geoffrey It was my mother's ambition for me. From – well, before I was born, I fancy. I – I always wanted to be an actor. Odd, isn't it? Though not so odd now I know that it's in the blood. (*Laughs.*)

Henry Acting is quite a dangerous profession in its own way, so I've always understood.

Geoffrey Perhaps more so for women.

32

Henry Ah yes. Quite. (*Pause.*) I seem to remember that Nelly – Mrs Wharton Robinson . . . There were two children?

Geoffrey I have a sister. She is married. She isn't at all interested in our mother and her previous life. She is perfectly settled, perfectly. For better or worse – So. So.

   Pause.

Henry May I ask further – I hope it's not an impertinence – my mother and your father, I mean my mother and your father – I mean – (*Laughs in embarrassment.*) Oh, what a shambles, I mean your father and your mother, your parents I mean, of course. Was it a happy marriage? Happy enough?

Geoffrey She was everything he could have wanted. They sang duets.

   Piano over, playing same tune as Dick and Nelly.

Henry Ah, well that's – that's –

   The song finishes. As they come to the end, Nelly turns her face up to George, who kisses it.

Nelly (*getting up – she is visibly pregnant*) Isn't it time for Assembly?

   George beams intensely at her. Little pause.

Dearest, you should hurry, I think.

George Shan't.

Nelly What?

George Shan't go to Assembly. Perkins can take it. I shall spend the morning here. With my family. My wife. My son. This one. (*Touches her stomach.*) That's my duty, as I see it. (*Laughs robustly.*)

Nelly But – but – what about the boys? You know how they begin to misbehave –

George Where is our Geoffrey? Is he still asleep?

Nelly No, dear. Jane has taken him for a walk.

George Well then – well then – We shall – why don't we – ?

Jane enters, carrying a package.

Jane (*making to give it to Nelly*) This has just come for you, ma'am.

George (*almost snatches it from her*) What is it? (*Examines it.*)

Nelly and Jane exchange worried looks, as Jane goes out.

Fanny's writing – you open it, and let's see what she's sent you.

Nelly I know what it is, it's her new novel – (*Putting it down.*) George, dearest, are you sure that Perkins will be all right? He has a rather feeble voice, and the smaller boys don't really respect him.

George The experience will do him good. You know, you girls are remarkable, remarkable. First Fanny's novels and Maria off to all corners of the earth, and published in the newspapers – but then I suppose you could say they're lucky in their husbands. I think of you sometimes, you know, the three of you – three girls, three little girls, so touched with a quality, a specialness.

34

He stands over her, beaming down intensely.

Nelly (*carefully*) Oh, I was too sickly and feeble a creature to feel at all special –

George (*interrupting*) Ah, but you were the one that the greatest man of his age took to himself as a godchild. He saw the specialness in you, did he not, being so special in himself – he a genius and you his muse?

Nelly Oh George, I've never made such a claim – I could never make such a claim. Good heavens! Have I ever made such a claim? I hope I haven't – he was a friend of the family who made himself my godfather because he was sorry for me, and he was such a long time ago – George, I can see that you're upset, what can be upsetting you?

George No, no. Happy. That's what I am, Elly.

He takes Nelly's hands.

Nelly (*puts her hand on his head*) Dearest George. But haven't you Latin after Assembly, with the Third?

George (*staring love at her, sinks to his knees*) I am the happiest man.

Nelly (*smiling anxiously down at him*) Dearest, dearest, darling George, what are you doing down there?

George I am worshipping my wife. My place is at her feet.

Nelly And hers is – is – in your arms. George, please do get up, dearest.

George I am your obedient George.

He begins to rise, stands smiling and nodding at her, bursts into tears.

Please forgive me, forgive me.

Nelly Forgive you? Forgive you for what?

George I don't know. (*Turns away, tries to compose himself.*) There's something I don't understand, I think there is.

Nelly (*takes his hand, leads him to chair, sits him down, sits down beside him*) You haven't been yourself for the last day or two. You have one of your unhappinesses coming on, I can feel it, so we must be careful, dearest, and not let you get – too fraught.

George No, no, it's not one of my unhappinesses, dearest Elly – the opposite, it's the opposite. I am overcome by my happiness, you see.

Nelly Ah! Well, that can only be good, George.

George Yes, wonderful, most wonderful! Except for the feeling that I have done nothing to deserve it. It is such a mystery to me, you see. Do you see?

Nelly No, George, I don't. What mystery, where is the mystery?

George You, oh my darling, oh my dearest, you are the mystery, Elly. You came into my life from nowhere – nowhere – to give me everything I'd ever hoped for, dreamed of! (*His voice is shaking.*)

Nelly This is very like one of your unhappinesses, George – when I have to keep telling you that I didn't come from nowhere. Not from nowhere, George. I didn't come from nowhere, you know very well where I came from, my darling.

George Tell me again. I love to hear you tell me, Elly.

Nelly (*slowly and urgently, as if to a child*) I came from Italy, from my sister Fanny's, where I had been living since fifteen because of my health, and then when I'd

36

quite recovered, when I was twenty-four, I came to stay with Maria, at Oxford. We met at her house. Where is the mystery in any of that, dearest? (*Attempting to laugh*.) It is the most ordinary way in the world for a young man to meet his future wife.

George Twenty-three. You were twenty-three.

Nelly Yes. There you are, you see. You remember it all perfectly clearly, I was twenty-three.

George stares at her intently.

Nelly George dearest – we are happy. We love each other. We have never loved anyone but each other – at least I haven't. (*Looks at him interrogatively*.)

George Oh Elly, my Elly – you know!

Nelly Well then?

George I wish I – I wish – oh, how I wish –

Nelly (*puts her finger to his lips*) You mustn't wish for more than we have, George.

George No, no, you're right. I mustn't do that. God might punish me.

Nelly God!

George Yes, of course God, Elly, who else but God? Why has He rewarded me, rewarded me instead of punishing me, for abandoning Him?

Nelly But you haven't abandoned Him. Never. When you decided not to become a vicar –

George (*tenderly*) Because you wouldn't marry me, Ellen, if I did.

Nelly But I was truthful with you. I could not have been your wife if you had been a vicar.

George So you say, so you say, but why? I still don't understand why, why, Elly?

Nelly Because I knew in my heart that He never intended me to be a vicar's wife. But I believe, from the moment we came to love each other, that He intended me to be your wife. How can you have abandoned Him? You are a man of faith, George. Parents wouldn't entrust their boys to us unless they believed that you are a man of faith.

George But supposing – supposing He has decided that He will no longer allow – that in giving you me – and that is why He makes everything I love, you and Geoff and the school, even this one – (*Touching her stomach.*) – seem wrong to me sometimes, and false? And I become full of dread and suspicions and I don't know what is to become of me – Oh, Elly, Elly, what am I to do?

Nelly George! George! What you must do – You mustn't do what you did last time, and neglect your duties. Please listen carefully, George. You have a class now. Is it another Latin class?

George Latin, yes.

Nelly Then you must go and give it. The boys depend upon you. Their parents depend upon you. You have a great responsibility to them. And to our little Geoffrey. And to this one. And to me. By fulfilling it you earn your happiness from God. You are a good man who deserves everything he has. I love you.

George You love me. Yes. I believe it. And I shall go about my duties straight. But first I kiss you, my most, most darling wife, my Ellen, and –

He clutches her desperately, kissing her. Nelly gazes despairingly over his shoulder, as if seeing Dick . . .

38

*. . . standing at a lectern, reading. He is full of energy –
in his pomp, gesticulating violent acts. This in dumb-
show. He reaches a climax, stands quivering with excited
horror, staring at his audience.*

Lights up. Church.

Dick And there was the body – mere flesh and blood, no
more – but such flesh, and so much blood!!

Sound of organ very low.

Nelly (*as if struggling*) Dear Father – Dear Father, who
art in –

*She stops herself, sits again, upset. The organ sound
has stopped. Complete silence.*

*An explosion of organ music, brief, very loud. Nelly
winces, shocked.*

Silence. Sound of footsteps.

*Benham appears, humming. He walks down the aisle
towards the door. He nods respectfully, not recognising
her in the dimness. Nelly gets up.*

Benham Mrs Robinson!

Nelly Mr Benham.

Benham Don't say you've been here while I was
thundering!

Nelly No – well, only a minute or two.

Benham A minute or two is all I allow myself. For
everyone else it's an eternity.

Nelly It suited my mood.

Benham Oh. Oh dear! A violent mood, then?

Nelly Well, I was thinking of the way things can change when one has – seems to have – a settled and – proper life – but you can never be sure that at any minute –

Benham There won't be a clap of thunder and a dreadful storm. Well, peace has returned, for good, I hope – let me leave you to it. Oh, but may I – may I take the liberty of reminding you of a promise you made to me the other month?

Nelly Promise?

Benham About Charles Dickens. I was showing you my collection – I'd just found a poster, do you recall, announcing a reading he was to give here, in Margate? In the town hall. And you told me about your most extraordinary relationship with him. Well, not extraordinary, I suppose, quite an ordinary one if it hadn't been with him, but he would make any relationship with himself extraordinary, from the point of view of a worshipper like myself – and you were good enough to say, well, to promise, that one day you'll try to describe him to me exactly as you remember him – anything you can remember of his conversation, any detail, even of his dress. I could write it down and show it to you, so that we'd be sure I have it correctly.

Nelly I was his mistress.

Benham I'm afraid I don't quite understand. You were, you say, I thought I heard you say –

Nelly So you see, I need – I need your guidance, Mr Benham. Your help.

Benham Of course. Indeed. But I still doubt – You said – Did you say that your were – mm –?

Nelly His mistress.

Benham (*stares at her*) But – but no. My dear Mrs Robinson – no. You must be using the word in a sense which is not familiar to me.

Nelly I'm sure we share the same sense.

Benham You were a child – just a child – when you knew him. When he died. You told me –

Nelly I am older than I led people to believe. Including George. I am a decade older than George.

Benham A decade! I see.

Nelly I have told no one else.

Benham As far as I'm concerned, Mrs Robinson, you have told no one. He seduced you, naturally.

Nelly I don't think so. It was as if I didn't quite know – I was very young – he made me confused. Yes, he confused me –

Benham Do you mean, he drugged you?

Nelly (*laughs slightly*) No, no. He wasn't – he wasn't – He was very kind to me. He loved me. I was more than just a – (*Gestures.*) He trusted me, my judgement. He read his work to me, every chapter as he wrote it, and then I read it through after he made changes –

Benham How honoured you must have felt.

Nelly Yes. I always honoured his genius. And served it.

Benham But the man, on the other hand –

Nelly (*after a pause*) I served him too.

Benham And honoured him?

Nelly I honoured his wishes.

Benham His desires.

Nelly It was what I undertook. He was always kind. As I've said. Kind. And he sacrificed so much for me.

Benham You sacrificed rather more for him, my dear, I think.

Nelly It was impossible not to love him. Everyone who knew him loved him. (*Pause.*) But his touch disgusted me. I hated my life with him.

Benham But not him?

Nelly Only when he touched me.

Benham And now you have a new life.

Nelly Do I deserve it? That is what I have come to ask you. Have I a right to it?

Benham Deserve? Have a right? But surely, my dear Mrs Robinson – we must accept what God has given us. We know what we deserve and have a right to by what we have.

Nelly I have learnt – am learning again – how to endure my shame. I had thought, with his death, my marriage, our child and the child to come, I should have some release And there was release. But now, with George, it is back, and I must endure it again. He blames me for persuading him away from his vocation, and of course I can't explain to him that I could never be a vicar's wife. My life would have been a lie, a daily lie, our lives ruined if it had been found out, and little Geoffrey's too, his life tainted for ever. And so of course I tell him that God intended him to be a headmaster, though he knows that really he has no gift for it – we are losing boys every term, our position is quite precarious, really very precarious – and the thing is, Mr Benham, whenever I seem to have him calmed down, the name of – of –

seems to pop up in him. Like a snake. I am desperate to help him – what can I do? Would it be better or worse for him if I told him the truth? It would free him – and free me with him. I could stop having to conceal and lie. We would live in honesty and openness – yes, the truth is always best, isn't it, Mr Benham? However painful.

Benham But you don't know what he would do with the truth, do you? If it made him angry it might also make him indiscreet – just once. He would only have to be careless or feel vengeful once – confide in just one person just once. Can you be sure he would be able to resist the just once, which would affect the fortunes of the school? The parents would almost certainly have the strongest moral objections – and you say they are already withdrawing.

Nelly It might be for the best. It might be for the best to give up the school. We could go away, abroad, start a school for English boys in Rome, start again from what we really are. If we failed then at least he would know why – he wouldn't need an explanation from God.

Benham If our only concern was George's welfare. (*Little pause.*) And yours. But we must not be selfish in order to be good. My dear, my dear, you wish to know what I believe? I believe you owe it to his memory not to soil his name. He is one of our greatest men, second only to Shakespeare if not actually equal to him – and in one respect, a most important respect, his superior. In his moral power. It lives on in the world through his works and through what is known of his character. Damage that, and you risk damaging the souls of all those who look to him to accompany them, guide them, on their paths through life. 'By their works shall ye know them' – by their works! No aspect of the life must be allowed to taint the works. No, my dear Mrs Robinson – Ellen –

you must carry the burden of your dreadful secret to the grave. As must I, now that I share it with you. Let me just say – say one thing – that may be in some way consolatory – that if there is that in your connection of which you should justly feel ashamed, there is also that of which you should justly feel proud. God has His purposes.

Nelly Thank you, Mr Benham. Good Mr Benham, and my friend.

Benham And your friend.

He takes Nelly's hand.

How is little Geoffrey?

Nelly He is very well, I thank God.

Benham Good, and you'll allow us the use of him for the Easter Pageant?

Nelly Of course. He adores dressing up.

Benham We'll make him into a bunny, perhaps. Or an egg.

Nelly He prefers to be ferocious.

Benham Ah. Then we'll find a reason for having a lion, shall we?

Nelly Yes, a lion. Perfect. Though I like him most of all to be a soldier.

Benham Then a soldier he shall be.

Nelly smiles radiantly at him, makes to go out. Benham watches her, then hurries off to desk, takes out a piece of paper, writes. Nelly is still onstage.

'My dear Wright, This commuanciation written in a state of extreme agitation. You remember I told you that I had

44

living in my parish a young woman who, as a child, had actually known Dickens and was in effect a kind of goddaughter to him, and you asked me if I could discover from her anything that would be of consequence in your projected biography. Well, my dear Wright, I have just had with this very woman the most extraordinary conversation, the contents of which I shall now entrust to you, and only you, knowing that you will understand the great responsibility this imposes on you as to how, and in what circumstances, you choose to disclose it to the world. My dear Wright, this woman, whose name is Ellen Robinson, and who is the wife of the headmaster of a boys' school here in Margate, was – so she claims, and I have no reason to doubt her, as she came to me distressed and bewildered and delivered her secret to me in the utmost confidence, and mark this, my dear Wright, her concern was less for herself than her husband, who is driving himself mad with jealousy of he knows not whom – this, my dear Wright, is the ghastly comedy of her situation –'

During this, lights up on desk, chair . . .

Office of Sir Henry.

Henry Yes, it may be odd, but I find myself very pleased. That your parents' marriage was a happy one.

Geoffrey Hah!

Henry Didn't you say?

Geoffrey I said she was everything he wanted. But that's not the same thing as saying that they were happy. Not at all.

Henry No. No, it isn't.

Geoffrey Where did he keep her?

Henry Keep her?

Geoffrey Yes.

Henry Well, they had a house in Slough. And then in Peckham. Or it may have been the other way around.

Geoffrey Slough?

Henry And Peckham.

Geoffrey Which part of Slough?

Henry I don't know, I never – visited – No one in the family ever visited.

Geoffrey (*nods*) To think that there I've been, in Slough, all this time – And Peckham, you say. Peckham and Slough. Strange places to keep a – a – my mother.

Henry I would imagine that he chose them because they could be reached easily by train. I remember in his last year or so how exhausted he was from the amount of travelling he did – from his readings. Manchester or Birmingham, then back to London, then to Slough or Peckham, then back to London and his office, then home to Gad's Hill, then to Slough, then off to Liverpool or Bristol for a reading. So much of his life seemed to be spent on a train.

Geoffrey But then – he liked trains, didn't he? All those pages he wrote about them, whole chapters in *Dombey and Son*. I remember how I admired – My mother used to imitate Bagstock, puff out her chest and put on a deep, blustery voice – and then tell me about how honoured as a little girl, to be his god – his god – daughter and – and you can feel how much – how much he loved going about – in trains.

He sits staring, rigid, as if in shock.

Henry Yes. Well, not after the dreadful business at Staplehurst Bridge, of course. (*Pause.*) Did your mother ever mention Staplehurst Bridge?

Geoffrey (*still staring*) Eh?

Henry The Paris Express – coming back from Paris – it crashed at Staplehurst Bridge. My father was in it, and so was your mother. And her mother, actually – your grandmother. All three of them were hurt – could have been killed. He climbed through the broken window of their carriage, was out and about pulling people out of the wreckage, the maimed, the dying. He was heroic, they all said, the newspapers. I don't think he ever quite got over it – the carnage – but it didn't stop him – Well, he had to, you know, he needed the trains to get back and forth for those damned readings – They were enough to kill him in themselves – we all begged him – begged him – but the readings and the trains, the trains and the readings together.

Geoffrey lets out an odd noise, like a laugh.

Mmm?

Geoffrey Mmm?

Henry Did you say something?

Geoffrey Oh, I was just thinking of the trains and the readings – and there my mother would be, waiting for him in Slough or Peckham between trains and readings. And then off again and back to Peckham or Slough. And off again – Yes, I can see how exhausting, how very exhausting. Now, I suppose, with the motor car, he'd be behind the wheel, much more restful for him, I should think. Drive straight up to the door. Straight up to her, at the door in Slough or Peckham.

Henry (*little pause, bewildered*) Yes, I suppose – um – with a motor car. But I can't quite see why you – where a motor car comes into it.

Geoffrey No. No, I don't know why either, the thought just popped into my head. I wonder whether – (*Little pause.*) Has it ever occurred to you to wonder whether – (*Makes to speak, checks himself, changes the subject.*) The readings. My mother used to say that it was one of her greatest sorrows that she'd been too young to go to them, that she'd never heard him read in public –

Henry Ah. Well. Of course she heard him.

Geoffrey Yes.

Henry It would have been hard for her to go to them, you know, especially at the end. It was hard for all of us – to see what it was doing to him – I sometimes hear him now. In my sleep. When I'm almost asleep, somewhere around then. His voice comes into my head – it starts me awake. My wife too. That is, I wake her because of the way I wake – with a cry – I'm sure there are many still alive who sometimes recall the experience in that sort of way, especially if they heard one of his last. He sometimes went beyond, far beyond, at the end –

Lights up on Dick at lectern, a book open before him. He is gesticulating violently, lurching slightly, a few words and phrases clear, others distorted, as in a nightmare.

Dick The noose was on his neck; tight as a bowstring and swift as the arrow it speeds (*garble*) and hung with his open knife clenched clenched clenched (*garble*) backwards and forwards on the parapet with a dismal

48

(*howling noise*) for the dead striking against a stone, a stone, dashed out his brain!! Dashed. Out. His. Dashed out his Braiiiins!

> *There is a long, eery silence, then cries and applause. Dick stands, swaying, mops his face, drinks water, bows, lurches slightly, bows again, then almost falls off the lectern and limps heavily away, mopping at his face and bowing. He stops, performs one last, unsteady bow, and lurches off.*

Thursday 9 June 1870. Off, the sound of a dog barking.

Lights up on Nelly, aged thirty-one, sitting at a table, reading a manuscript.

Jane (*enters*) Nelly, he's coming. He's just crossing the field.

Nelly Who?

> *Jane sees Nelly's face, laughs.*

The master, indeed. And doesn't Quilp know it. Do let him out, dear – You know he needs to be the first with a greeting. (*Puts manuscript carefully away.*)

Jane (*as she goes out*) He's limping badly. Shall I help him with his bag?

Nelly No, put the water on.

Jane I've put it on.

Nelly Then open the door for Quilp.

> *Jane goes out. Sound of Quilp being released, running, yapping excitedly. Nelly goes to window, stares out.*

49

Sound of Dick's voice and yapping coming closer, then in the hallway.

Dick (*outside the door*) No, no, you can't come in here, old Quilp, you're too demanding, and I want all the attention.

Dick enters. He is now fifty-eight. He is carrying a heavy briefcase and a stick, and is limping heavily.

All the attention.

He puts down his bag, holds out his arms.

Nelly (*goes into his arms*) You always get all the attention – far more than is good for you.

Dick I know – but it's too late now to stop it. People are in the habit. It would be unfair and unkind to try –

He stops, aware of Nelly's scrutiny.

Mouse? Your whiskers – (*Touching her mouth.*) – are twitching.

Nelly takes his finger away from her mouth, then goes to the table, pours him a large brandy, carries it to a small table beside his chair. Dick sits, grimaces with pain.

Nelly Are they worse?

Dick I don't believe there's a writer in London that doesn't have them. Tennyson, for example, all he talks about – people visit him expecting music from his lips, instead they get details of his haemorrhoids, and in prose! Well, better than in verse, I suppose. And Wilkie, Wilkie, just the other night he was saying he kept putting off his new novel, couldn't face the thought of sitting at his desk for more than five minutes – (*Adjusts himself.*)

Nelly Your cheek is swollen.

Dick Yes, damned tooth. I took a spoonful of laudanum. Nearly took some before the reading, when it was raging, but didn't, in case I fell asleep just when I was getting into – (*Checks himself.*) – my stride. (*Drinks deeply, gratefully.*) I saw you there. At least I thought I saw you. It was most curious, though – the sensation I had in my stomach, a slight dizziness, as when I saw you for the first time – She was the twin of you as you were then.

Nelly As I was then? Well, perhaps it was the ghost of me as I was then.

Dick Now I see you properly, properly, I think she was neither twin nor ghost, not pretty enough, not anything enough. And the man she was sitting with didn't look at all like me – he had a droopy, listless manner and a cough. He coughed during 'The Signalman', and followed it with a wheeze, I caught his eye, gave him a piercing look and a quick snarl, he gave me a friendly little nod and a smile.

Nelly And what else did you read?

Dick Oh, I started with Mrs Lirriper, the Paul scene from *Dombey and Son*, David's thrashing, Bumble, Pumblechook, the usual repertoire to the usual success – hall full, people standing, leaning through the windows, hanging from the rafters, protruding from the cellars, triumph, triumph, triumph, the whole of Sheffield still reeling from my coming thither and my going thence. Particularly my going thence, lamentations mingled with the applause, triumph, triumph – despair.

Nelly And did you do Pickwick?

Dick I did.

Nelly And did you say Pickwick?

Dick I said it very clearly.

Nelly What?

Dick His name.

Nelly Whose name?

Dick His. (*Little pause.*) Pickswick.

Nelly Pickswick.

Dick No. (*Little pause.*) Piskwick.

Nelly Piskwick.

Dick Is it so?

Nelly Can't you hear it?

Dick I hear – his name. When you say it and I say it I hear the same name. Very well, it is so. Pick – Pick – (*Stops.*) I'll ask Emsworth what it means, he'll probably tell me it's quite common in gentlemen of a certain age, especially those who insist on showing themselves off to the world –

Jane enters, carrying a large jug and a bowl.

Dick Ah, Jane.

Jane (*putting the bowl down, pours hot water in*) Sir.

Dick Have you given up smiling?

Jane No, sir.

Nelly She worries about you.

Dick I know. She's very kind. But when I'm at home there's no need to worry, is there?

Jane No, sir.

Dick So you can smile. (*Looks at her.*)

52

Jane smiles.

Now I am at home. Thank you, Jane.

Jane goes out. There is a pause. Nelly refills his glass.

Yes, Mouse. Home. Home.

Nelly You murdered, didn't you?

Dick Murdered? (*Laughs.*)

Nelly You read the scene from *Oliver Twist*. That you promised me you would never read. Ever. Again.

Dick Oh, that murder! No, Mouse, no – how could I, when I made such a promise to you? And to Georgina. And to Dolby. And promised Forster. And promised Wilkie. In fact I can't think of anyone I didn't promise – except the audience, of course. To whom I could scarcely say – (*Puts his arm over his chest.*) – I do solemnly swear and promise that I will not murder this evening. At least in front of you. Nancy is safe. Bill Sikes is safe. And so are you. And so am I.

Nelly Look at you. You are exhausted.

Dick I was. (*Drinks.*) I feel fresher by the second.

He takes her hand, raises it to his lips. She puts her hand on his head.

Henry's office.

Geoffrey Were there any children?

Henry (*confused*) Children?

Geoffrey Do we perhaps have any half-brothers or sisters, you and I?

53

Henry (*pause*) Well, of course there's no way of knowing for sure. There are always these claimants – bogus, as I told you when I thought you might be one of them, but never the slightest shred of evidence –

Geoffrey I was an easy birth. She used to joke about it. How many children did he have by your mother?

Henry stares at him.

Excuse me. (*Little pause.*) If I may ask.

Henry Ten. If you include poor little Dora. She died very young.

Geoffrey Thirteen years together. A man who had fathered ten children and a woman who had an easy birth when she was forty. Perhaps he had them killed.

Henry (*looks at him, shocked*) My father – my father could never – whatever his faults, he could never –

Geoffrey Or put them out as foundlings. Who can say?

Henry But surely you knew your mother as I knew my father – how can you imagine –?

Geoffrey No sir, no sir, excuse me, but you don't understand. I don't know my mother as you knew your father. You not only knew his past but what he was doing – doing with my – my – She lied to me all my life. If she was capable of that, what else was she capable of? (*Little pause.*) And my father – my wretched father – There was a noise he made, a dreadful howl, like a dog – a dog grieving. Dear Jane, our maid, would put me on her knee and have me stick my fingers in my ears until he'd stopped, stopped his howling, but then there would be his voice, limping on and on and on, and sobs, and Ma speaking so sweetly and gently, never letting him hear her exhaustion and never letting me see her despair.

'The world is a hard place for a man like your father,' she'd say. 'He was born for the Church, his nature was to serve his God, but it wasn't to be.' I never asked why it wasn't to be, thinking that his tendency to howl and weep were enough to prevent him from being anything at all, even a clergyman. But if he guessed – or knew – who had taken his wife when she was a young woman, a girl of seventeen, a child, a child, really – took her and kept her as his mistress and had babies by her which he – which he'd had killed, or farmed out to orphanages – (*Stands up, trembling with anger.*) What manner of man was this man? What manner of man, this Charles Dickens?

Slough. Living room. Dick and Nelly As before, Dick holding Nelly's hand, Nelly's hand on Dick's head. Dick groans, shifts uncomfortably, bends towards his bad foot.

Nelly I'll do it.

Dick No, no, I can –

He reaches down to his boot, undoes a lace, seems about to topple sideways, rights himself. Nelly bends, undoes his boot laces. Takes off his boot. Dick yelps.

Nelly Oh, I'm sorry, Nunky. Sorry.

Dick Not you – the gout! The gout's to blame! (*Laughs.*)

With great care, Nelly peels off sock, under which are layers of bandage which she begins to unwind.

Nelly (*peeling off the last of the bandages*) Oh, look at this, look at this! (*Holding his naked foot.*) And it used to be such a beautiful foot! Such a springy, bouncy,

carry-you-anywhere sort of foot. How could you do this
to it?

Dick It's not my fault, Nell, you mustn't blame me for
the wear and tear –

Nelly Whom am I to blame then, myself?

Dick No, no, nature, it's nature's wear and tear. Natural,
Mouse, natural wear. Natural tear. As a man gets older –
and older – and older – (*He seems to drift away.*)

Nelly You're not old. You're fifty-eight. That's not old.
You're in the middle of a new novel. I thank God for
Edwin Drood.

Dick God? Thank Him for it? Why?

Nelly Because you won't let yourself die before you
finish it.

Dick Don't you mean He won't let me die before I finish
it? But I'm putting my all into it. All that I have. And a
bit extra. Just for you, my Mouse, because you are my
muse and my Mouse – (*Reaches a hand towards her.*)
And you're in my heart as I write.

Nelly But it's to be a murder story, isn't it?

Dick It's a love story, with murder in it. And the murder
has love in it – (*Settling back.*) Aaah, Nell, how good
you are to me!

Nelly says nothing. After a pause:

Yes, I am beginning to feel very well again. (*Little pause.*)
Now, shall we sing? I've been back at least twenty
minutes and we still haven't sung.

Nelly In a minute perhaps. I have a headache.

She sits down, looks at Dick.

Dick Oh, poor Mouse. Did you ride this morning?

Nelly A little trot – then it began to drizzle.

Dick Oh, poor Mouse. Poor, poor Mouse. (*Little pause. He seems to drift off.*) No, no, all is settled, all is settled.

Nelly What do you mean?

Dick What? Oh – oh. I was just remembering an odd thing. On the way back from Sheffield I suddenly had the sensation that the carriage was slipping down to the left, for a second I was convinced that the train had left the tracks – and then when I began to feel safe I started thinking of the dead – the wounded – the cries – and then I made myself think – think that here we are, Mouse, you and I, we came through, we are alive. We still have each other. We still have each other. All is settled in spite of it, was my thought. Is my thought now. (*Smiles at her.*)

Nelly And it's a very comforting thought.

She goes to the piano, tinkles. Stops. Starts again.

But what I remember now, what I keep thinking of now, is how I was thrown one way and hurt myself, and Mama was thrown another way and broke her arm, and you – you were out and about saving people's lives and your reputation – (*Jangles the keyboard.*) – your reputation!

Dick I did all that I could. All that I could think to do – Oh Nell, here we are, here we are, you and I – (*Reaches out a hand.*)

Nelly (*after a pause*) You lied to me.

Dick Lied? Lied about what?

Nelly You read the scene. You murdered. I know you did. I can tell. That's why you're like this. When you left you looked healthy – almost healthy – and you come back, you come back – and you promised. You promised me!

Dick I didn't want to. I didn't. But I had no choice. They were expecting it. But I did it very quietly. Calmly and quietly. There was almost no excitement – I kept the fuss and drama to a minimum.

Nelly No, you didn't. You were ferocious. You were terrifying. The audience cried out when you beat Nancy upon her upturned face – when you seized the heavy club and struck her down – they moaned aloud – and the look on your face – (*Contorting her face.*) And struck her down! And then you took the dog and dashed his brains out! And what next? Why not yourself? Dashed your own brains out – Yes, it would have been like that – a dashing of yourself to death for the entertainment of your public – their loyal servant – to the end. And beyond – and yet you promised me!

She goes out of the room.

Dick Nell! Nell!

He struggles to his feet, stands breathing heavily, in pain.

Nelly (*entering*) What will become of me if you go on like this! You will die and what will become of me? Do you ever think of that?

A pause.

Dick I'm sorry. I couldn't resist, I wished to see the terror on their faces, and their pity, so it was vanity, I did it from vanity, we both know, but it was for the very last time. How could I do it again?

He holds out his arms. He is trembling.

Look at me, Mouse.

58

Nelly I can't bear to look at you, I can't bear it. (*Turning her head away.*) What you do to yourself –! Oh – oh – (*She turns, looks at him.*) Oh, Nunky, lie down, you must lie down.

She goes to him, takes him by the arm, helps him back on to the sofa. She arranges his body.

There you are. Now rest.

Dick (*takes her hand, carries it to his beard, strokes his beard with it*) What do you make of it now?

Nelly (*kisses him quickly on the lips, twines her fingers in his beard, blows into his beard*) Oh, how uncared for it is, like a neglected bush, so tangled, and rough –

Dick I never touch it, between going away and coming back. I wouldn't dare, it belongs to you – such as it is, such as it is.

Drowsily, he catches her hand, kisses it.

And yet it was you – you who asked me – wasn't it?

Nelly What? Asked you what?

Dick When we walked that time – our first time – Condaster.

Nelly Doncaster, do you mean?

Dick If you could feel my beard.

Nelly I had to feel your face, to make sure you had one, that you weren't a devil underneath it all.

Dick A devil! Hah! I was a poor forked animal –

Nelly Perhaps that's the same thing.

Dick Not to itself it isn't. To itself it's a poor forked – (*Gestures.*) And look on the poor forked now. Recumbent, groaning on a sofa –

Nelly Not even your love can stir it.

Dick I didn't say that, Mouse. But of course whether the spectacle of it can stir you –

Nelly To what? To my mousy devotions?

She kisses him on the tip of the nose.

There. Does that hurt?

Dick No. It soothes.

Nelly (*runs her hand gently down his body, stops at his crotch, presses slightly*) Soothes?

Dick No.

Nelly Oh – (*Alarmed.*) Hurts then?

Dick (*catches her hand, puts it back*) It enlivens. Brings me back to life.

Nelly Oh, any woman's hand can do that. If you shut your eyes you can make it any hand you want it to be.

Dick It could only ever be your hand. You always have my soul in your hand, to do as you like with. That is how I know your hand.

He takes her hand, presses it against his crotch.

Through my soul.

Nelly So it is your soul I press like this – like this – like this –

She is becoming almost vicious in pressing her hand. Dick lies back, lets out a cry, ghastly in its combination of lust and pain. They look into each other's faces. Nelly forces her hand up to Dick's face.

Nelly My fortune, please.

Dick You know I can't – not any more. Not of someone I love so deeply.

Nelly Of someone you love so deeply? Someone? Like me, you mean? And why not of someone like me you love so deeply?

Dick Because our lives are inseparable. I would be telling my own fortune too, and no man can do that.

Nelly Well, we can tell our pasts, can't we? Let us see what's happened to us since you took possession of me. (*Pulls his hand back, compares them.*) Yours is such a wavy line, full of crosses and clutters, here – you see – while mine just goes on in a drear straight line except for the losses, the two sad little losses – could these be they? This little little lump here, and this here – do they show on your hand – well, you have more, here and here and here and here and here – so those could be all your sad little losses, my two just two among them – which would they be? It's hard to tell, they're lost among all the others that belong to you alone, well, to you and someone else that you loved once, must have done, loved her indeed, else how could you have so many losses marked on your palm?

Dick Nelly, Nelly, please –

Nelly Now where is Staplehurst Bridge? Staplehurst Bridge should be identical on both our palms. How would a train crash show? And dead people, and people who'd lost arms and legs and children – how would their screams show? Can we see Staplehurst Bridge on yours –? Yes, here, this looks like a crash, and this on mine – yes, almost the same, look, your two lines and my two, and at the beginning here, like a stretch of railway track, and on it the Paris Express, from the heart of Paris to the heart of London. You used to say how you loved it, there it goes – (*Runs a finger along his palm.*) Chuff-chuff-chuff-chuff-chuff – chuff – closer to Staplehurst Bridge and closer – (*Getting faster and faster.*) Chuff-chuff-chuff – chuff – Crash! Crash! (*Pause, studying his hand.*) What does this mean here, and here, does it mean – chuff-chuff-chuff, me thrown one way and hurting myself, and Mama thrown another way and breaking her arm, and here you are, here, look at you! Scrambling through the window, pushing away all the broken glass, and then your voice – (*Imitating Dick's voice.*) 'There are two ladies in there! Sharing the compartment, I don't know who they are, but two ladies – two ladies in the carriage who've been hurt – Do see to them while I see to all these others, please look after the two unfortunate ladies I happened to be sharing a carriage with.'

Dick attempts to struggle to his feet.

What are you doing! (*Holding him down.*) Be still, lie still!

Dick I will not!

He makes a titanic effort, struggles out of her grasp, stands upright. He is shaking.

There! Here I am!

Nelly Yes, yes. There you are, here you are – now lie down again, Nunky –

Dick What for, what for, Nell? Look at me – see me – see what I've come to. You always talk about what you've given – look what I've given. This is all that's left of me, all.

Nelly Oh, Nunky, I was only playing. (*Takes his arm.*) Oh, you're trembling – lie down, please lie down, and – and we shall read your next chapter of *Edwin Drood* together, shall we?

Dick What, what, who?

Nelly Edwin Drood, Nunky.

Dick What?

Nelly Your novel, Nunky. *Edwin Drood.*

Dick (*after a pause, speaking carefully but emotionally*)
Dread and dread are dood, stepfoots and I fog my dreet
and swearest have pittle litty on her monkey. Nouse.
(*Pause. Stares at her bewildered.*) Mell? Nouse?

Nelly Oh Nunky – Nunky –

> *She pulls him gently to the sofa, settles him, is careful
> to keep his foot safe.*

There, there, back where you belong. (*Looks at him.*)
Oh, look at you, look at you, look at you, Nunky,
Nunky, Nunky – oh –

> *She kisses him on the forehead, then on the tip of his
> nose, then on his beard. Kneels, takes his foot, kisses it.*

Dick Oh. Oh mlovingmell – Nunce – Nunce –

> *He gives a cry, then shudders, goes still.*

Nelly (*after a moment lifts her head*) Nunky? Nunky?
(*Gets up, looks down at him.*) What is it? Oh. Oh,
Nunky – Oh please don't, oh please don't be – (*Taking
his hand, clasping it tightly, kneels beside him.*) Jane!
Jane!

> *Jane enters.*
>
> *Nelly clasps Dick to her.*
>
> *Jane comes and puts her hand on Nelly's shoulder.*
>
> *They stay on stage, as if in a tableau.*

Henry's office.

Geoffrey I apologise for my outburst.

Henry No need, no need – I quite see how upsetting this must be for you.

Geoffrey Until the day he died. Isn't that what you said. That she was with him until the day he died?

Henry She was, yes.

Geoffrey Did he – did he die in her arms then? As my father did? In her arms?

Henry No, no, not quite. But he was with your mother when he had his stroke. He was barely conscious, sometimes not even that, but she managed to get him into a carriage and all the way to Georgina at Gad's Hill, quite alone and by herself she did that. She was determined, for his sake and for the sake of his family, that he should die in his own home. And be universally known to have died there. (*Pause.*) It must have been a frightful business for her, frightful. None of us sufficiently showed our gratitude at the time, perhaps. Whatever your feelings I'd like you to believe that his love for her, and hers for him, was very great.

Geoffrey And if I did believe it, would it be a consolation, do you think?

Henry No. No, perhaps not. (*Pause.*) And to tell you the truth – the truth for me – is that though I am so much older than you, some things remain as fresh as if we were the same age. Let me tell you that – I once heard Mama – when she thought she was alone in the house – It was a sort – something like a, well, not a howling, no, but a noise, such a noise – Yes. And at that moment I wished them both dead, your mother and my father, for being the cause of such – such a noise from my mother.

They sit in silence.

Geoffrey (*gets up*) You've been most kind. And honourable. May I say honourable?

Henry (*also getting up*) I hope, in due course, that you'll come to forgive your mother, if not my father. After all, you've already lived so much life, been through a war with great distinction, obviously, and now have your bookshop in Slough –

Geoffrey (*shakes his head*) No. Oh no. No.

Henry I beg your pardon?

Geoffrey I shan't go back to Slough. Never back to Slough. I shall move to London, and – and I believe I will apply for parts.

Henry Parts?

Geoffrey In the theatre. As I said, I only went into the army because my mother wanted me to. Really, I longed to be an actor. It's in the blood, is it not?

Henry Well, yes, I suppose. But it might be a bit late –

Geoffrey Oh, I expect I shall have to start very low on the tree, but there are certain character types which would come to me naturally, I believe. Of course I'll take a few lessons first.

Henry Well, I'll follow your career with as much interest as if – you were – (*He holds out his hand.*) – some sort of relation. If a distant one.

Geoffrey Thank you, sir, thank you.

They shake hands, hands still clasped as if in a tableau as . . .

Lights down on both tableaux.

Curtain.